IMAGES OF ENGLAND

WALLSEND

IMAGES OF ENGLAND

WALLSEND

KEN HUTCHINSON

First published 2005
Reprinted 2006

Reprinted in 2013 by
The History Press
The Mill, Brimscombe Port,
Stroud, Gloucestershire, GL5 2QG
www.thehistorypress.co.uk

© Ken Hutchinson, 2013

The right of Ken Hutchinson, to be identified as the Author
of this work has been asserted in accordance with the
Copyrights, Designs and Patents Act 1988.

All rights reserved. No part of this book may be reprinted
or reproduced or utilised in any form or by any electronic,
mechanical or other means, now known or hereafter invented,
including photocopying and recording, or in any information
storage or retrieval system, without the permission in writing
from the Publishers.

British Library Cataloguing in Publication Data.
A catalogue record for this book is available from the British Library.

ISBN 9780 7524 3424 7

Typesetting and origination by
Tempus Publishing Limited.
Printed in Great Britain.

Contents

	Acknowledgements	6
	Introduction	7
one	High Street	9
two	Village Green	37
three	Wallsend Parks	47
four	Churches and schools	63
five	Streets and buildings	75
six	Shipbuilding	93
seven	Mining	107
eight	Roman Wallsend	117

Acknowledgements

This book has been produced on behalf of Wallsend Local History Society. Thanks are due to a large number of people, too many to list here, who have helped me over the years to develop a keen interest in the history of my hometown. Eric Hollerton (Local Studies Librarian) and Geoff Woodward (Curator of Segedunum Roman Fort, Baths & Museum) both put my name forward to the publishers as a potential compiler for this volume because of my continued involvement with Wallsend Local History Society and my long career with North Tyneside Council Planning Section. Special thanks are given to my wife Pauline who helped type up the captions and who, together with my sons Peter and David, has made many sacrifices over the years as I pursued my interest in Wallsend and built up my collection of information and photographs.

Many of the photographs used in this book have come from the collections of North Tyneside Council Libraries Local Studies Centre and Wallsend Local History Society. A number were donated by individuals such as Malcolm Dunn and Winifred Wynn, but there are too many to record here, though all deserve special thanks and will hopefully get great pleasure from seeing them featured in the book. Wallsend Local History Society was established to promote the town's heritage in 1973 and a large number of individuals have given up a lot of their own time over the years producing the Society's archive of photographs and documents which I have used to produce this book. Sadly, a number have died and others are no longer active in the Society, but they all deserve to be mentioned and include: Vin Wallace, Maimie Wallace, George Hopewell, Edmund Hall, John and Sheenah Stephenson, Dorothy Hall, Gordon Crennell, Bill Baxter, Joyce Smith, Beatrice Clark, Alan Baxter, Ann Baxter, Shelia Davidson, Don Price, Ken Hall, Mike Forrester, Shelia Aitken, Tom Jones, Bill Griffiths, Harry and Evelyn Hoy, Peter McGrath, Dave Thurlbeck, Jimmy Robinson, Harry Domoney, Alf Senior, Ian Brown, Margaret Thompson, Jimmy Ashurst, Jack Wylie, Rose Henderson, Iain Watson, Billy Mole and many more. Thanks are also due to staff at Segedunum Roman Fort, Baths & Museum for their help and encouragement; to all in North Tyneside Council's Environment, Regeneration and Housing Directorate, in particular the Planning Section; and to the Libraries Division of the Cultural Services Directorate, especially Eric Hollerton, Alan Hildrew and Doreen London.

If anyone has any old photographs of Wallsend, especially those featuring streets or buildings that have disappeared, or special events, school photographs, team photographs etc., please allow Wallsend Local History Society or the Local Study Centre to copy them and they may even appear in a future publication. In addition, please let either organization know if you find any inaccuracies or omissions in the book, for which the author would like to apologize, as some dates have had to be estimated and some information on people and buildings featured is unconfirmed.

Wallsend Local History Society was established in 1973 to promote and preserve the heritage of Wallsend. The Society meets every second Monday of the month at 7.00 p.m. in the Memorial Hall on Station Road, Wallsend, and illustrated talks are given on a wide range of subjects linked to local history. Visitors and new members are always welcome.

Introduction

Wallsend is famous throughout the world for a number of reasons and derives its name from being the terminus of Hadrian's Wall, which is a World Heritage Site. In 1835, Wallsend Colliery had the then worst recorded mining disaster when 102 lives were lost. Swan Hunter's were one of the worlds leading shipbuilders, building the famous *Mauretania* and *Ark Royal* to name just two famous vessels. The world-famous singer Sting was also born in Wallsend. This book features interesting snapshots of Wallsend's past, together with illustrations of how the town has developed over time. The majority of photographs used are from the original township of Wallsend, south of the Coast Road, and exclude Willington, Willington Quay, Howdon, Hadrian Park and Battle Hill which later became part of present-day Wallsend.

Wallsend began as the Roman fort of Segedunum (meaning 'Strong Fort') in the year AD 126. The fort was built four years after the wall had originally ended at Newcastle (Pons Ailus), presumably because the river could still be crossed by enemies between the present settlements of Newcastle and Wallsend. It was built on a hill overlooking the River Tyne with commanding views along the Bill Reach to the south-west and the Long Reach to the east. The wall was extended to Wallsend to a narrower width than the original wall built to the west from Newcastle, proving that it was an afterthought. A civilian settlement (Vicus) grew up outside the fort on the protected south-west side extending to the river, where a bathhouse was built to serve the community.

After more than three centuries, the Romans abandoned the fort when they left Britain and presumably people continued to occupy the site for some time after this. As the site on the riverside was vulnerable to raids from Vikings and Danes, it is thought that the fort and town was eventually abandoned in favour of a new settlement away from the river, around the present Wallsend village green. The village of Wallsend was made up of a number of farmhouses built around the village green and the surrounding fields were used for agriculture. Around the year 1150, Holy Cross church was built on a site above the present Burn Closes to the east to serve the two villages of Wallsend and Willington (close to the site of the present St Mary's church on Churchill Street).

Little changed for centuries in Wallsend, with the main settlement surrounding the village green. A few buildings were built on the side of the Newcastle to North Shields turnpike road (on the line of the present High Street and Church Bank) including the original Coach and Horses inn and Rose inn which were both built as coaching inns.

In 1778, coal mining commenced in Wallsend, which transformed the town from an agricultural village to an industrial town, with the main pits (A and B Pits) being developed around the site of Segedunum Fort. Other main pits were developed to the west of the village green (C Pit) and to the south-east of the turnpike road (G Pit), as well as miners cottages being built close to these pits and gradually extending outwards. Wallsend's coal was soon to become famous for its high quality and it commanded the highest prices in the London markets, which led to other collieries also calling their produce 'Wallsend Coal' to get the best prices. Wallsend Colliery was also famous for having one of the most respected mining engineers, John Buddle, based there. Sir Humphrey Davey developed his famous safety lamp at Wallsend, but unfortunately this could not prevent the mining disaster which took place at Wallsend on 18 June 1835, which was the worst-recorded such incident of its time.

As the town grew around the coal mines, Wallsend Green also saw a number of changes as large country houses were developed by merchants from Newcastle such as Wallsend Hall, The Grange, The Red House and The White House. The Village School was also established on The Green. Holy Cross church fell into disrepair in the late 1700s and in 1809 a new parish church, St Peter's, was built on Church Bank. The Old Village School was used for church services during this period.

Coal was loaded onto Collier ships at Wallsend and other industries also developed along the riverbank at Wallsend, including chemical works and shipbuilding. Shipbuilding eventually came to dominate the riverside, with Swan Hunter's and Wigham Richardson, North East Marine and Wallsend Slipway occupying vast sites in Wallsend and building hundreds of ships over the years, giving the town its worldwide reputation. Housing developed close to the riverside to accommodate the rapidly growing workforce, and at the same time Wallsend High Street developed as the main shopping and entertainment centre for the town with a large number of pubs opening.

Wallsend became an Urban District Council in 1901 and elected John Boyd as the first mayor and Wallsend Town Hall was built in 1908. In 1910 Wallsend Borough was extended to include Willington, Willington Quay, Howdon, Bigges Main and Rising Sun Colliery. In 1974 Wallsend Borough became part of North Tyneside Council. Wallsend continued to expand outwards and new churches and schools were built as housing estates expanded northwards over the present Coast Road and beyond around the Rising Sun Colliery which was opened in 1912 to the north of the town. In 1966 the Forum Shopping Centre was developed and from the 1980s the traditional shipbuilding industries declined, being replaced by industries connected to the offshore oil industry.

Wallsend continues to change and adjust to new pressures including the development of the major landmark, Segedunum Roman Fort, Bathhouse and Museum, which opened in 2000 to celebrate Wallsend's rich heritage for the next generations to enjoy.

Further information on Wallsend can be obtained from Richardson's excellent *History of the Parish of Wallsend*, *Where the Wall Ends* and *The Wallsend Colliery Pit Disaster 18th June 1835*, which are all available from North Tyneside Council libraries.

Ken Hutchinson
September 2004

one

High Street

The Duke of York Inn, High Street West, c. 1967. This is the first pub on the High Street when travelling from Newcastle. Wallsend's boundary follows the centre line of Shields Road until it meets High Street West, before turning south down The Avenue opposite the inn. The present building was built in the early 1900s, replacing an earlier inn of the same name.

This image features a cleared site to the east of the Duke of York Inn, High Street West, in 1974. The old shops on High Street West have just been removed before new housing is built. Opposite the Duke of York Inn on the corner of The Avenue is the old police station building, which had been converted to housing. The Tait family lived in one of these houses fronting on to The Avenue, which still had three of the original cells and an exercise yard, complete with bars to windows and reinforced doors.

Here High Street West looking west is viewed from the corner of Border Road, *c.* 1925. The newsagents at No. 68 High Street West on the corner of Border Road is owned by Alexander Brook, later to become Siddle's newsagency. Beyond the shop, the Queens Head public house and the Anchor Inn can also be seen.

High Street West looking east from the corner of Border Road, *c.* 1905. The trams passed through Wallsend between Gosforth and North Shields from 1902 onwards, and followed the line of the old Coxlodge wagon way through the former village of Bigges Main, where the Wallsend Sports Centre was built.

Above: This photograph of High Street West looks east on the corner of Hedley Street and was taken around 1925. Greenwell's grocery store is on the corner of Hedley Street and beyond is the Robin Hood Inn.

Left: Robin Hood Inn, High Street West, *c.* 1967. This inn was rebuilt in 1913 and records exist of a Robin Hood Inn existing as far back as 1828. It has changed names a number of times in recent years, including being called Chadwick's and The Ship.

Taken before the Ritz Cinema was built in 1939 to replace the buildings immediately to the west of the Black Bull, this image is from the 1920s and looks east onto High Street West.

Robin Hood Inn and the bingo club, High Street West, in 1985. The former Ritz Cinema has here been converted to a bingo hall and the longestablished Alsop's Bike Shop was still going strong with vacant units beside it.

Backley's bakery on 120 High Street West was one of two bakery shops on Wallsend High Street owned by Robert L. Blackburn, seen here *c.* 1930.

High Street West, looking east from the Black Bull Hotel, *c.* 1913. All the buildings beyond the Black Bull Hotel have now been demolished and replaced by the Forum Shopping Centre.

The Ship Hotel (with the large clock) on High Street West, photographed in 1913. The hotel occupies the corner of Carville Road, with the Cooperative Stores on the opposite corner.

The demolition of the Ship Hotel on High Street West in 1985 while looking west from the Forum. The Ship Hotel and Constitutional Club were redeveloped to build a new Lloyds Bank and shop units.

Ainsworth fishmonger's shop, High Street West, in the 1930s, getting prepared for the Christmas rush with a large number of geese and turkeys on display. The shop was situated close to Station Road on the north side and was later cleared to make way for the Forum in the early 1960s.

High Street West looking east from Atkinson Street, c. 1910. The pawnbroker's sign is clearly visible on the northern side of the street.

These shops were doomed to be demolished on High Street West in 1963 to make way for the Forum Shopping Centre. Ruddick's greengrocers at Nos 27-29 High Street West was previously known as John Milne Fruiterer, named after the man who set it up around 1906.

Hadrian Supplies Stores, No. 31 High Street West, 1963. This self-service grocery was the forerunner to today's supermarkets.

The junction of Station Road and High Street, looking east, in 1963. Boots, Graftons and Woolworths occupy the corner sites.

This was High Street West, with the north side looking west in 1965, shortly before all of these properties were demolished to make way for the Forum Shopping Centre. The Station Hotel was known as The Penny Wet, as it used to open at 6.30 a.m. to supply shipyard workers with a coffee and rum purchased for 1d.

This is High Street West from Station Road junction, looking west during the late 1930s. Martins Bank occupies the corner site and was built before 1909, when it was originally the North Eastern Banking Co.

The junction of High Street West and Station Road, looking west, c. 1905. Three different modes of transport are shown – tram, car and horse and cart. Wallsend Café and Athenaeum, which was built in 1883, dominates the corner.

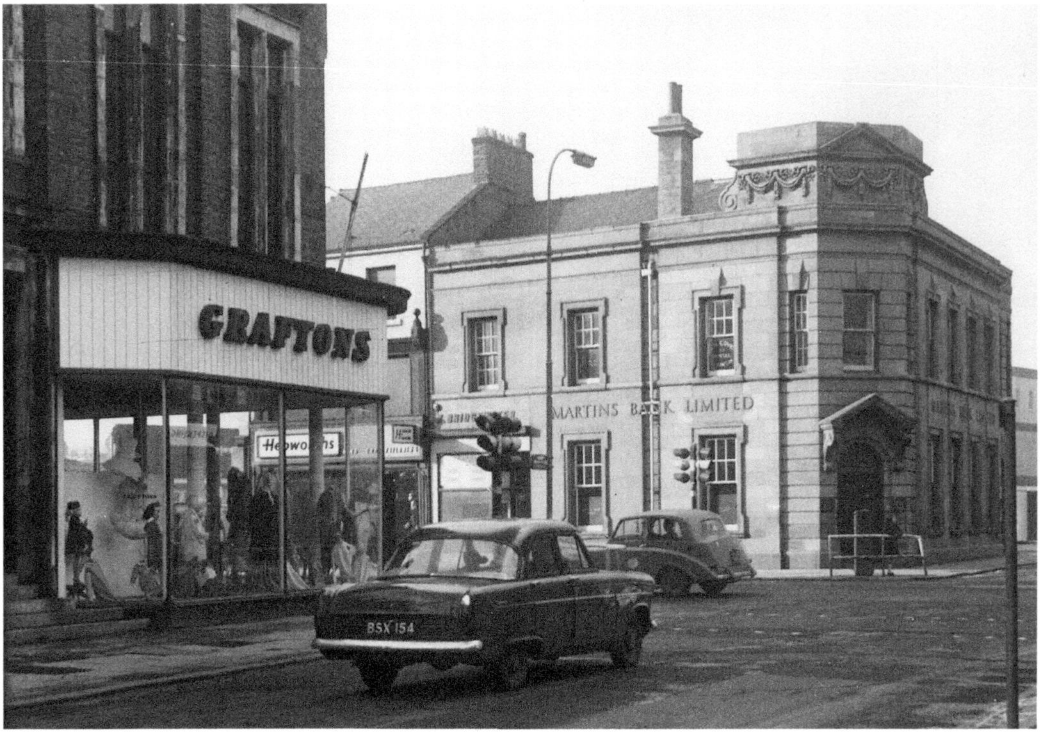
GRAFTONS
Hepworths
MARTINS BANK LIMITED
BSX 154

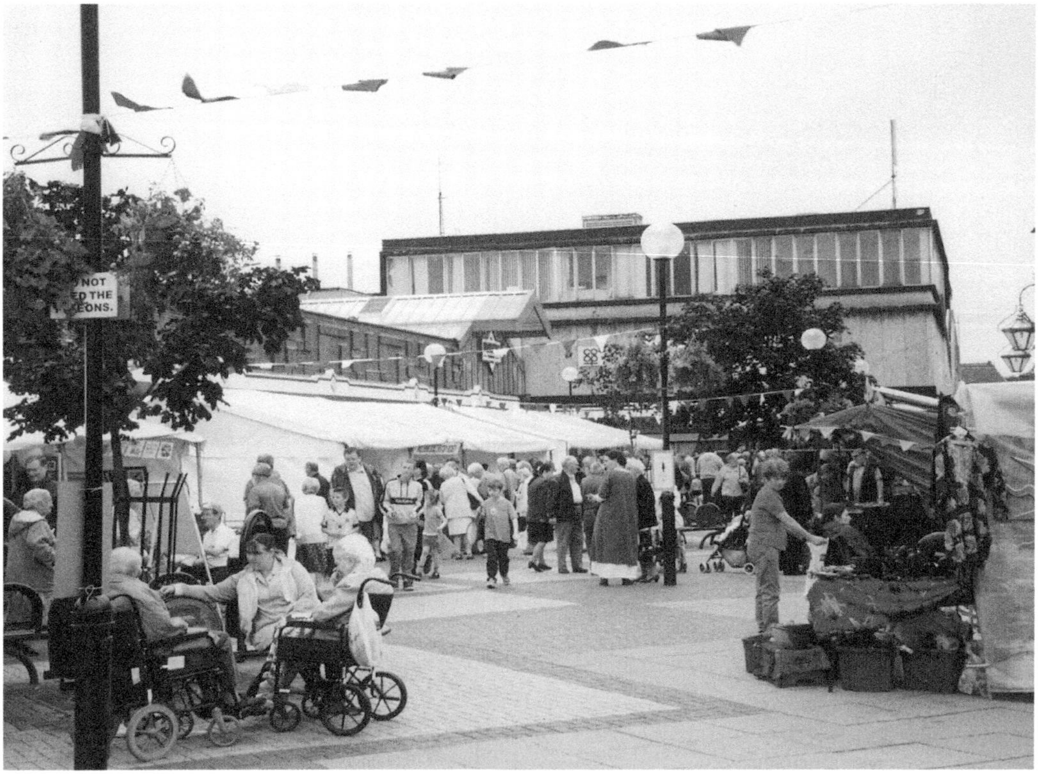
O NOT
ED THE
EONS.

F.M. Boon, chemist, at No. 261 Station Road during the late 1940s. Miss Boon had set up her own shop in Station Road from 1929 but eventually took over her father's shop on the High Street after the war.

Opposite above: This photograph was taken at the junction of Station Road and High Street West in 1967 shortly before Martins Bank was demolished. Graftons ladies fashion store occupied the corner site for decades.

Opposite below: Wallsend Festival, the Forum, on Saturday 6 July 2002. The Anson public house is on the right and the Cooperative Stores in the background. Wallsend Local History Society's stall is in the centre of the picture to the left of the lamp-post.

High Street East, looking east from the junction with Station Road, c. 1910. Boots Chemist and Central Buildings are very prominent on the corner site with Station Road. The site currently occupied by Woolworths appears to be vacant and is being used for advertising.

High Street East, looking east from Station Road junction, in the 1930s. The traffic is so quiet that the policeman has time to offer advice to the driver in the middle of the junction.

Percy Robert Garrod's fishmonger's shop at No. 130 High Street East, c. 1928. The shop worker photographed is Frederick Ainsworth, who worked in the shop between 1922 and 1931 before opening his own shop at No. 21 High Street West in 1932.

High Street East, looking west from Sycamore Street junction, c. 1903. The Zion Methodist church occupies the site on the corner of Station Road, shortly after to be replaced by Central Buildings and Boots Chemist. The site opposite is used for advertisements before the bank was built.

High Street East, looking west from Sycamore Street, c. 1908. This photograph was taken soon after Central Buildings and the bank were constructed.

High Street East, looking east from Station Road, c. 1916. The junction of Woodbine Avenue is on the left and John Richardson's drapery shop, established in 1902, is on the right.

Fred Jewitt, butcher's shop, at No. 76 High Street East, in the 1930s. The Jewitt family had a long association with Wallsend and also had other shops in Benton Way, Buddle Street and Station Road. Fred Jewitt is pictured second from the right and his brother Mark is on the far right.

Winters' Supply Stores at No. 86 High Street East, c. 1927. This was one of a number of Winters' stores, which were grocers and provision dealers. The company was established in 1916 by Leonard J. Winters.

High Street East, looking east, from Sycamore Street, in the 1930s. The Bon Marche store occupies most of the block between Woodbine Avenue and Laburnum Avenue. The shop developed from a draper's store, established by Mrs Lilley Ann Smith in 1904, who chose the name Bon Marche because the shop next door was already called Smith's.

High Street East, looking west from Sycamore Street, *c.* 1902. On the right is the junction with Woodbine Avenue.

Above: Borough Theatre, High Street East, *c.* 1909. The theatre opened in 1909 and was built by the owner, Cllr Joseph Duffy, who was elected Mayor of Wallsend in November 1909. He died in July 1910 during his term of office. The theatre became the Gaumont Cinema in 1946 and closed in 1960. It was later reopened as a bingo hall in 1962.

Right: The interior of the Borough Theatre – an artist's impression, *c.* 1909. The building was designed by Messrs Davison and James. The top of the bill on the first performance was Miss Harriet Vernon, who featured in *Emblems, or Why Britannia Rules the Waves.*

The Borough Theatre, *c.* 1911. A large poster on Park Road advertises forthcoming attractions.

The Boro bingo club in 1985. A mural has been painted on the gable wall of the building opposite, on the corner of Park Road and High Street East.

Above: High Street East, looking west from Ferndale Avenue, 21 July 1926. This scene follows the declaration of the results of a poll to nominate Margaret Grace Bondfield to stand as MP for Wallsend on behalf of the Labour Party.

Right: R.H.S. Craw, family butcher's shop on No. 204 High Street East, was listed in local directories from 1909 and is pictured here around 1910, but was given up by 1918 when Robert Henry Stroud Craw was killed in action during the First World War.

Above: The New Winning Tavern on High Street East, taken in the late 1960s, was rebuilt in 1894 and is the last pub on Wallsend High Street before the road name changes to Church Bank.

Left: This painting shows William Boyd, who was elected Alderman and first Mayor of Wallsend in 1901. He was Managing Director of Wallsend Slipway Co. He had previously been a member of Wallsend Local Board of Health from 1878 and chairman from 1879 till 1894 when he became the first chairman of the newly established District Council. The portrait, painted by Ralph Hedley, was presented to him by the borough in 1903.

Town Hall, Wallsend, c. 1920. Viewed from the south, children are gathered outside the main entrance and the original wrought-iron railings are clearly visible at the front of the building.

Municipal buildings, fire station and baths, High Street East, *c.* 1910. This was opened on Wednesday 16 September 1908 at a total cost of £15,557 12s 11d by Alderman G.A. Allan, Chairman of the Municipal Buildings Committee.

Opposite above: This meeting in the Council Chamber of Wallsend Town Hall on 15 May 1912 was being held to enroll Samuel Turner Harrison as the third Freeman of the borough. He worked at North East Marine and from 1885 was elected to the Local Board of Health. He was also elected as an Alderman of Wallsend Borough Council and became the fourth Mayor of Wallsend in 1904. The photograph shows the original seating arrangement in the chamber where Mr Harrison is seen signing papers, seated in a chair, on the right of the photograph.

Opposite below: Wallsend Town Hall is seen here in 1951 during Jubilee celebrations to commemorate the fiftieth anniversary of the formation of the Borough of Wallsend in February 1901. The building was decorated and floodlit for the celebrations.

Queen Elizabeth II visits Wallsend Town Hall on 29 October 1954. The photograph was taken in the Council Chamber during a visit to Wallsend whilst Her Majesty was signing the visitors book.

The public baths at the junction of Lawson Street and Vine Street, Wallsend, c. 1912. The large building on the corner housed the main swimming pool. The main entrance to the baths and swimming pool was on Lawson Street.

The swimming bath, Wallsend, c. 1912. The building was designed by F.W. Liddle and Percy L. Browne of Newcastle and had a pool of 100ft by 30ft as well as slipper baths, vapour baths and Russian baths. It was opened on 12 June 1912.

Coach and Horses Inn, High Street East, c. 1901. It is thought that there has been a Coach and Horses Inn on this site since before 1739, when it was recorded as being situated on the North Shields Turnpike Road between Newcastle and North Shields.

Coach and Horses Hotel, High Street East, c. 1908. The date stone on the building is 1902, which would indicate that the building pre-dates Wallsend Town Hall. The upper floors of the hotel are now used as offices and meeting rooms for the council. The present building replaced the earlier Coach and Horses Inn that closed in 1901.

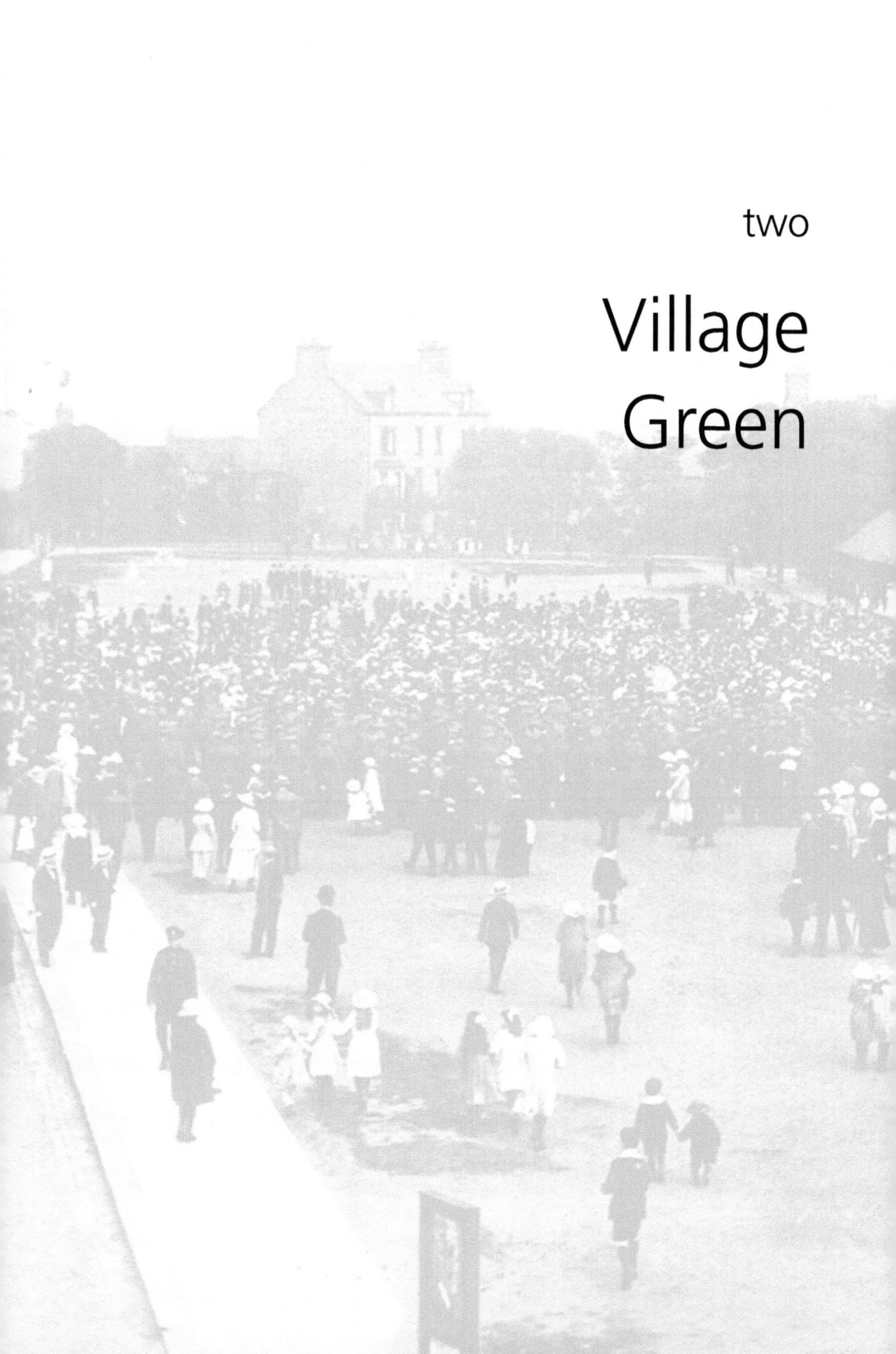

two

Village Green

The Green looking south-west towards The Villa and The White House, c. 1890. The Villa was built around 1850. The White House, here partly hidden by trees, was one of a number of large houses built around the village green by the major landowners in Wallsend. The building originally had three reception rooms, two kitchens, five bedrooms, two attics and a wine cellar. It also had a large stable, coach houses, large pleasure grounds and a fish pond.

The Green, looking east to the Old School House and Dene House, c. 1900. The Old School House was occupied by generations of the Mordue family. Joseph Mordue became schoolmaster in 1776 and was also parish clerk, and his son Joseph took over as schoolmaster in 1818. He also built a brewery behind the school on Crow Bank, which was closed in 1879. Dene House was built by Frank Mordue, on what was the Old School House garden, in the late 1800s. The buildings to the right of the photograph are East and West Villas, built in the late 1870s.

The Green, Wallsend, c. 1910. This view is taken from outside properties on Hawthorn Villas, looking east across the private road, towards the Lodge at Wallsend Hall. The Old School House is visible through the trees.

Elm Terrace, Wallsend Green, c. 1910. This was formerly the site of North Farm, which was pulled down in 1871 to build Elm Terrace.

Above: Wallsend Hall on the village green, in the 1920s. The Hall has always been the largest and most imposing building on The Green. It was built by the Moncaster family in the early 1700s after the previous occupants, the Hindmarch family, had died out. William Clark took over Wallsend Hall in 1790 and he was infamous for removing the roof of Holy Cross church in the late 1700s, which led to the church's ruin. The Old School House had to double up as a church until St Peter's church was opened in 1809. In 1856 Robert Richardson Dees, a Newcastle solicitor, bought The Hall and in 1897 he gave fourteen acres of land, located at the site of the former C Pit, for a public park which was named after him. Robert Irwin Dees later inherited The Hall and moved there in 1909, when he was Mayor of Wallsend. Sir G.B. Hunter bought The Hall in 1914 and in 1916 presented the house and grounds to the mayor and corporation. In the 1920s The Hall became the Wallsend and Willington Quay Infirmary and Maternity Hospital; it was later known as the Hunter Memorial Hospital.

Above: The photograph shows, from the left, Alderman Thomas Connell, mayor, his daughter Miss Margaret Connell, Mr John Shields Wylie, deputy mayor with Mrs Margaret Wylie, deputy mayoress and numerous guests beyond in the Civic Hall, 1954.

Above: The crowds have gathered on Wallsend Green in 1918 to celebrate the end of the First World War.

Opposite below: Wallsend Civic Hall and Hospital in 1985. In the 1950s, an extension was built to the north east of The Hall to form the Civic Hall, which provides function rooms for the council and various other bodies.

Crow Bank, Wallsend, around 1900. This road leads from the village green to the Burn Closes and Holy Cross church.

Jasmine House and Cross House at the top of Crow Bank in 1985. The Old School House was converted into two houses when the school closed, and both are listed buildings.

The Village Green Farm occupied the site to the east of The Villa on the south side of The Green, seen here in the 1950s; it was demolished and replaced by Grange Close in the early 1960s. The farm was originally in the hands of the Allan family and Dame Allan established a school for poor children in Newcastle paid for by the rents from the farm.

Wallsend Green looking west, c. 1903. Park Villas and Hawthorn Villas are seen in the distance and were built after 1897 to replace The Red House, which had been demolished in the late 1890s.

Allen Memorial church, 1985. The original spire on the church had to be removed as it had become unsafe and was too costly to replace. The church was opened in 1904 to replace a Zion Chapel that was situated on the corner of High Street East and Station Road. It was named after John Allen and his wife who were great supporters of the church. He was a prominent chemical manufacturer who had chemical works on the riverside at Wallsend.

The Careers Office, Park Road, in 1985. It had previously been used as Wallsend Library. The Castner Kellner Alkali Co. was set up in 1906 on the riverside. The company originally erected this building in 1910, as the Castner Memorial Institute, for use by the workers of the company.

The Stadium and government offices, The Green, in 1988. This photograph looks east, and was taken shortly before the demolition of The Stadium building to make way for new housing known as White House Mews. The government offices were demolished later and replaced by Hunters Close.

The Stadium, The Green, looking west from The Villa in 1985. The Stadium was originally built as a skating rink, then used as a factory to build aeroplanes (Zeppelins) during the First World War and between 1919 to 1920 it was used as a boxing hall. In 1922 the Daimler Co. Ltd set up a car factory in the building. It was later used as a training workshop for the Ministry of Works, before being converted into a large paper store for government records.

The Stadium from the rear in 1985, seen from the corner of Coronation Street and North View.

The Stadium from the rear looking west, 1985. On the right are Morgan Villas and in the background on Park Road is the St Columba's church Parochial Hall.

three

Wallsend Parks

Bowling Green, Wallsend Park, *c.* 1908. This view is south towards the recently constructed houses in North Road and the Allen Memorial church, with its original spire. Richardson Dees Park was opened on 4 June 1900 and named after the Newcastle solicitor Robert Richardson Dees who lived in Wallsend Hall. He donated the land, which was formerly the C Pit of Wallsend Colliery, to the town.

The Duffy Memorial Fountain, Wallsend Park, c. 1912. Mr Joseph Duffy was a local builder and brick-yard owner who was also Mayor of Wallsend in 1909 and he died in 1910, while in office. The memorial fountain was unveiled in 1912.

The Park, Wallsend, in the 1940s. This photograph was taken from just inside the entrance, off North Road, looking towards the greenhouse with Park View behind.

The Park, Wallsend, in the 1930s. Looking west towards Park View.

The Lake, Wallsend Park, *c.* 1910. The photographer is looking east towards Kings Road, which is beyond the fence.

Wallsend Park looking east towards Kings Road, c. 1905.

The lake in Wallsend public park looking west, in the 1940s.

Part of the old Roman wall, Wallsend Park, in the 1930s. When excavations took place in Swan and Hunter's yard in 1903, preparing for the building of the *Mauretania*, part of the branch wall from the Roman fort of Segedunum was found. This was photographed and recorded by Walter S. Corder and parts were taken away and rebuilt in Wallsend Park on the north side, close to Kings Road.

Roman wall, public park, Wallsend, in the 1940s. The wall has either been moved and rebuilt, or has been repaired and re-pointed when compared with the previous photograph.

Right: Roman wall, in Hall Grounds below Lily Bank in 1985. This section of the branch wall had been removed from Wallsend Park and rebuilt in the Hall Grounds.

Below: Stones taken from the East Gate of Segedunum Roman Fort and a section of the Roman wall in the Hall Grounds with an eastern view of Queens Terrace in the background, 1985. All the stones were taken back to their original sites when Segedunum Roman Museum opened in 2000.

Band stand, Wallsend Park, 1985. A local brass band entertains visitors during an event in Richardson Dees Park.

Kings Road from Wallsend Park, *c.* 1913. Looking north, the two properties on the left are the first houses to be built in High View, before the street itself was built. The large building in the centre is Highfield, the former home of Robert Irwin Dees, who was mayor in 1908.

Kings Road South, looking north, in the 1920s. On the left is Wallsend Park and on the right is the Hall Grounds and the corner of Queens Terrace.

The Dene in Wallsend Park around 1910. This postcard contains little detail to pinpoint its exact location.

Burn Closes, Wallsend, looking west from the foot of Church Bank, *c.* 1910. Many children are visible playing in The Burn, possibly on a Sunday School outing.

Opposite above: Killingworth wagon way Bridge, Burn Closes, *c.* 1900. The wagon way led from Killingworth Colliery to the Killingworth Staith on the River Tyne to the west of North East Marine Engineering works. The bridge was demolished after 1940.

Opposite below: The base of Wallsend Pump, Wallsend Dene, 1996. This stone structure, with stairs leading up to the platform, was used to supply water to the people of Wallsend from cast-iron pumps situated at the southern side of the structure. Just over the hill behind lie the remains of Holy Cross church, built around 1150.

Looking east on Burn Closes, Wallsend, c. 1910. Haggies Rope Works can be seen extending from the bottom of Church Bank to the Willington Viaduct.

New Bridge, Burn Closes, Wallsend, looking west from Church Bank c. 1913. This was built by William Thomas Wier of Howdon between 1912-1913 for Wallsend and Northumberland Councils, to enable new housing and a new cemetery to be built in the Holy Cross area.

Bridge, Burn Closes, Wallsend, *c.* 1914. Looking south-east towards Church Bank, this photograph still has a number of terraced houses concealing St Peter's church from view.

Church Bank, Wallsend-on-Tyne, from Rosehill, c. 1905. Carling's cottage and stables can be seen on the right, close to the burn itself.

Church Bank, Wallsend, from Rosehill, c. 1935. The new Rose Inn, built in 1913, and the secondary school can be seen at the top of the bank.

Rosehill, Wallsend-on-Tyne, from Church Bank, *c.* 1905. The entrance to St Peter's cemetery is on the right and the cast-iron railings around the cemetery are also visible. The old Rose Inn can be seen in the centre of the picture beyond the tram.

The old Rose Inn, Willington-on-Tyne, *c.* 1911. The inn closed on 6 February 1913 and the licence transferred to the new building. The Dobson family were the tenants for many years and Thomas Dobson's name is visible above the door on the right.

Burn Closes from Rosehill, Wallsend, c. 1920. The new Rose Inn and Burn Closes Bridge, which both opened in 1913, feature prominently in this postcard.

four

Churches and Schools

Holy Cross church, c.1900. The church at Holy Cross was built around 1150 to serve the villages of Wallsend and Willington and was situated between them, overlooking Wallsend Dene and Wallsend Burn Closes. It was used up until 1797 when the roof was taken off for repairs and never replaced. The church became a ruin and deteriorated badly, until the ruins were consolidated in 1909 and a fence erected around them.

Holy Cross church from an engraving, c. 1810. M.A. Richardson published a number of stories in his table book of legends in 1846. One story concerned a meeting of witches at Holy Cross church that was discovered by a member of the Deleval family returning from Newcastle one night. He found witches dissecting a corpse of a woman and putting the parts in a cauldron suspended from bell ropes. He caught one of the witches and took her back to Seaton Deleval, where she was tried and sentenced to death by burning at the stake on Seaton Sands.

Holy Cross church in 1995. This photograph looks south with the consolidated church in the foreground and St Peter's church in the background.

St Peter's church, c. 1900. The original St Peter's church was consecrated on 27 April 1809. It was a plain building with a semicircular east end and a square tower at the west end, with a modest spire within the crenellated tower. The present building is the result of extensive rebuilding in 1892, when it was changed into the perpendicular style. The spire was taken down and the church was extensively altered and extended.

St Peter's rectory, c. 1970. The new vicarage was built in 1852 to take the place of the old vicarage on The Green. It was later demolished in the 1980s and replaced by a modern building and sheltered housing.

St Peter's church AFC 1908/09. The incumbent of the church, at this time, was Revd Charles Edward Osborne.

St Andrew's church, *c.* 1910. Situated on the corner of Border Road and Warwick Road. It was demolished in the late 1990s and replaced by housing.

St Luke's church, *c.* 1909. Looking south from Station Road

St Luke's church and vicarage, Station Road, *c.* 1909. St Luke's church opened in 1887 and the vicarage in 1903. They were built to serve the rapidly growing town.

Hadrian United Methodist AFC, Wallsend, 1913/14. The United Methodist church was on Hadrian Road beside Davy Bank. The team played in the Tyneside Amateur League. The team photograph was taken at the village pump in Wallsend Dene, close to their training field. From left to right, Back Row: Billy Park, goalkeeper. Middle row: Billy Griffiths, George Cook, Billy Simpson, Dick Batey, Billy Engels. Front row: Bob Cresswell, Jackie Davis, 'Chicken' Boyle, Arthur Brannigan, Donald McQuarrie, Sandy McQuade (trainer).

Brunswick church on the corner of Laburnum Avenue and High Street East, c. 1920. The original Wesleyan church and Sunday schools were built between 1901-1902 to accommodate the 800 worshippers and 500 pupils. It became known as the Brunswick church in 1932. It was declared redundant in 1967 and demolished. Flats now occupy the site.

Richardson Dees School, High Street East, Wallsend, c. 1910. The school was opened on 24 February 1902 by the Mayor of Wallsend, Alderman William Boyd.

Richardson Dees First School building on Boyd Road, c. 1985. The school was being demolished to make way for playing fields at the same time as the main school was being refurbished.

St Columba's Roman Catholic Schools, Hedley Street, in 1974, shortly before the schools were demolished. The upper floor was occupied by St Columba's Secondary Modern School. The headmaster was Mr A.R. Hutchinson, the author's father, who occupied the office on the first floor of the flat-roofed block to the right. The lower floor was used by St Columba's Junior School. This is where, in the early 1960s, the author shared a classroom with Gordon Sumner, later to be known as 'Sting'.

St Peter's School, Church Bank, *c.* 1910. This was originally built in 1833 and subsequently extended in 1874 and 1905.

St Peter's School, Church Bank, March 1994. The school was demolished in 1995 and replaced by sheltered housing. The original date stone from 1833 was salvaged and built into the stone wall on the church side and reads *Deo et Pauperibus* which means 'For God and His Poor'.

Secondary Schools, Wallsend, *c.* 1920. They opened on 23 September 1914 as the Secondary School and Technical Institute. It later became Wallsend Grammar School and then Burnside High School in 1969.

Wallsend Secondary School for Boys; staff and schoolchildren seen here in September 1920.

Burnside High School, March 1994. Taken from the tower of St Peter's church, this photograph shows the former Grammar School in the foreground, the former Technical School immediately behind it and the former Central Schools to the right.

Western School and red phone box, Forrest Road, 1985. The photograph is taken from West Street looking north. The school was demolished in 2004 following the opening of the new school on Rutland Road.

Old Carville School, 1980, taken shortly before it was demolished to provide playing fields for the new school, seen in the foreground.

five

Streets and Buildings

Benton Way Victory Tea in 1919. The street party was held to celebrate the end of the First World War.

Elton Street West Victory Tea, September 1919. The lady and gentleman seated at the front are Nina and George Gray, who was a local butcher with a shop in Hedley Street. The lady to the right, wearing a spotted apron, is given as Sophie Turnbull, and Alice Bryson is said to be visible in the background.

Glover's Row, Wallsend, in the 1930s. This terrace was built in the 1860s for the workers of John Glover's Alkali Factory on the riverside. It was situated to the south of High Street East and to the east of Oak Grove. It was replaced by industrial buildings to the north of the Metro line.

Ferndale Avenue, in the 1920s. The view incorporates Durham Street West looking north and the large house on the corner later became a doctor's surgery.

Captured here is Philiphaugh in the 1920s. The street is on the boundary with Newcastle. On the allotments facing the houses, a Roman altar was found in 1892 and the inscription on the altar proved that the Roman name for Wallsend was Segedunum.

Elton Street in the early 1960s. This looks south-west over cleared ground to the rear of High Street West, with the Ritz Cinema in the centre. An old garage occupies the site to the rear of St Columba's Schools (to the left of the road sign). The Forum Shopping Centre was built on the vacant site.

This picture of Nos 130-138 Neptune Road, Wallsend, was taken on 2 October 1973 by Planning Department staff for the Westfield Terrace Compulsory Purchase Order, 1972. This was prior to the widening of Neptune Road.

Nos 2-12 Neptune Road, 2 October 1973. This photograph was taken shortly before the properties were demolished.

Neptune Road, Wallsend, c. 1920. This is looking west, with Neptune House on the left. Built in 1908, it is now a listed building and was originally built as an office for the Walker & Wallsend Union Gas Co., then later used by Thermal Syndicate Ltd and more recently as a carers centre. The eye-catching OXO advert is on the corner of a shop on the Avenue.

Wallsend Trade Procession in 1925. The horse and cart pictured features the products of Thermal Syndicate Ltd. It is thought that the parade was in support of the newly opened hospital on The Green.

Shiney Row, North Road, *c.* 1910. The old miners' cottages are in the foreground, with the Buddle Schools in the background, behind the roofline.

Wanless Street, *c.* 1937. Taken shortly before demolition, this photograph looks south towards High Street West, with R. Wilkinson's butcher's shop visible in the distance.

Opposite above: The Turner's Buildings, which were situated behind the Black Bull on High Street West, in the 1930s. They were thought to have been named after John Turner of West Farm.

Opposite below: Wallsend Cooperative Stores, North Road, *c.* 1970 situated on the corner of Lisle Street, this building was later converted into a residential home.

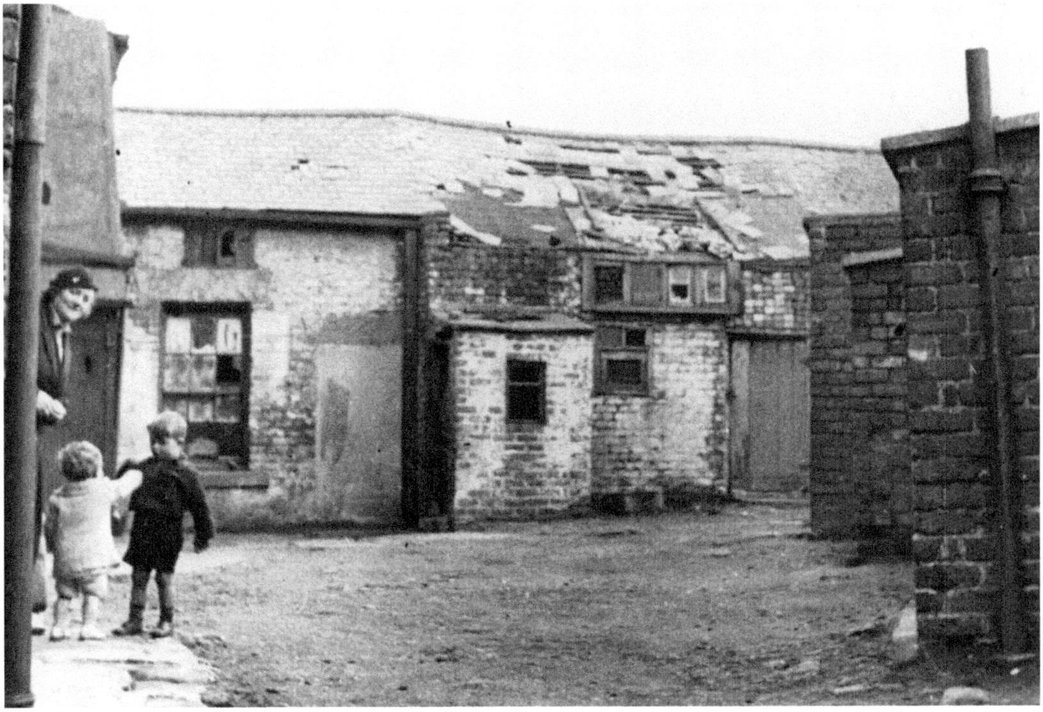

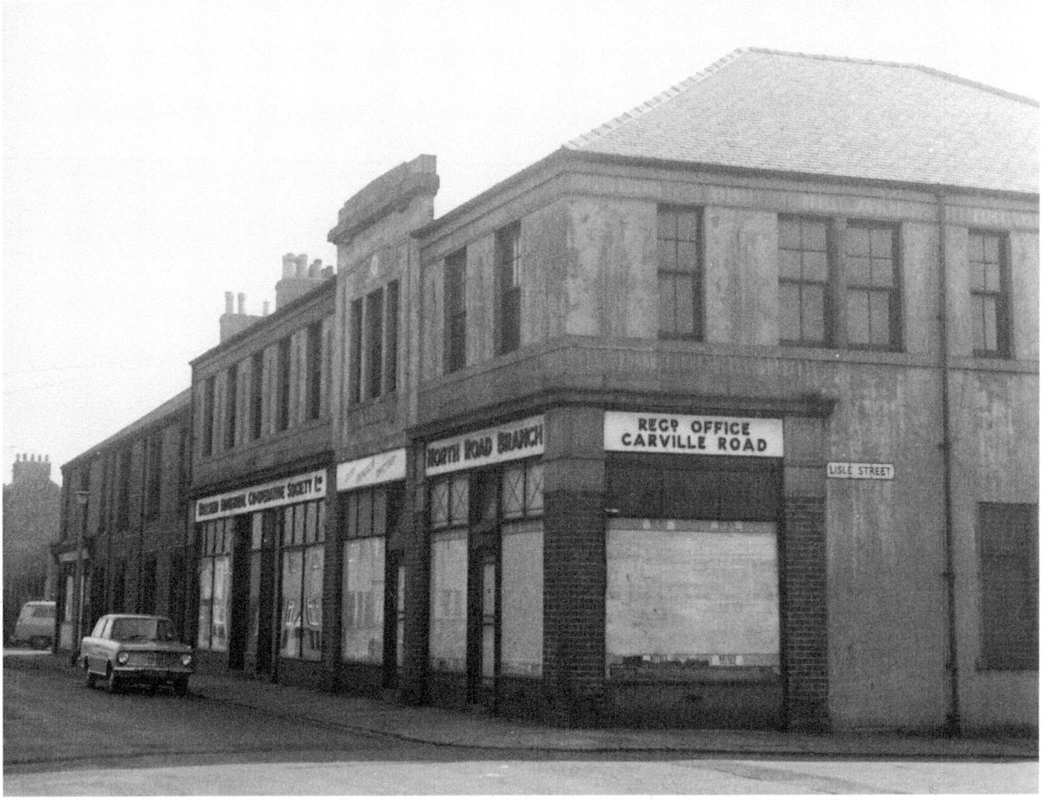
Co-operative Society Ld
North Road Branch
REGD OFFICE
CARVILLE ROAD
LISLE STREET

Wallsend Motor Co., High Street East/Lime Kiln Road, c. 1930. This was one of the earliest motor companies in Wallsend.

Portugal Place, c. 1940. A horse and cart being used to salvage paper, bottles and jars for the war effort can be seen outside the corporation depot.

Warwick Road, early 1930s. This image shows the corporation vehicles parked on Warwick Road. In the background is the spire of St Andrew's Presbyterian church on Border Road.

Carville Station, Hadrian Road, in the 1960s. The station was built on the Riverside line, which was opened in 1879, while the station itself only opened on 3 August 1891. The Riverside line was later closed in July 1973.

The Swinburne Brass Works, Hadrian Road, c. 1984. Situated on the north side of Hadrian Road and to the east of Park Road, Swinburne Brass Works was established in 1892 and finally shut its doors in the 1980s.

North Road, Wallsend, c. 1920, with Allen Memorial church seen behind.

This photograph features Park View, which overlooks Richardson Dees Park, *c.* 1920.

Sunningdale Avenue, Wallsend, *c.* 1920. The street is incorrectly named Sunnydale Avenue in the postcard. The view is from Coronation Street.

Laburnum Avenue, *c.* 1920. We are looking north from High Street East, with the shadow of the spire of the Brunswick chapel in the foreground.

This photograph is of Equitable Street in 1974. Looking south, the Cooperative laundry is on the left with Gordon Square stretching beyond. In the background is the spire of St Andrew's church on Border Road.

Hedley Street, 1974. The gaze of the camera is north to Equitable Street, with St Columba's Schools fence on the right and, again, Gordon Square remains visible beyond.

Gordon Square, 1974. The viewpoint, from the rear of High Street West towards Thames Street and Hedley Street, shows Gordon Square in the centre and St Columba's Schools to the right. The Cooperative laundry chimney can also be seen above Gordon Square.

Davy Inn, Davy Bank, in the 1960s. Situated at the bottom of Davy Bank, the Davy Inn was reputed to have anchorage rings attached to the wall of the pub. These rings were said to be used by customers to secure boats on the river running past the pub, prior to the river being narrowed in the 1850s. The Mordue family, from the Old School House on The Green, were licensees until 1921. They sold beer from their brewery, on Crow Bank, in the pub during the 1800s.

Opposite above: Commercial Hotel, Denham Terrace, in 1967. Situated just north of the B Pit at Segedunum, it opened in 1896 and was ultimately demolished in the 1970s.

Opposite below: The Carville Hotel on Carville Road, taken here during the 1930s, was earlier built in 1893 as 'a first class hotel, especially adapted for the accommodation of visitors'.

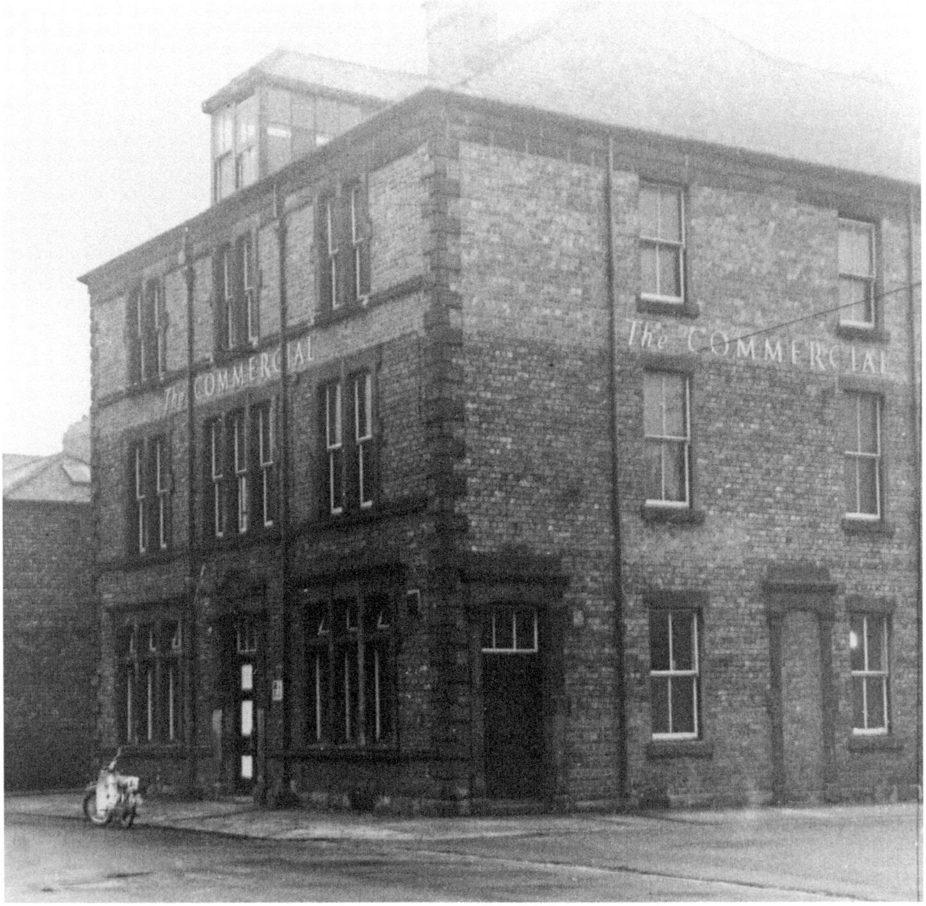
The COMMERCIAL
The COMMERCIAL

OXO
No. 116 Long Row, Wallsend.

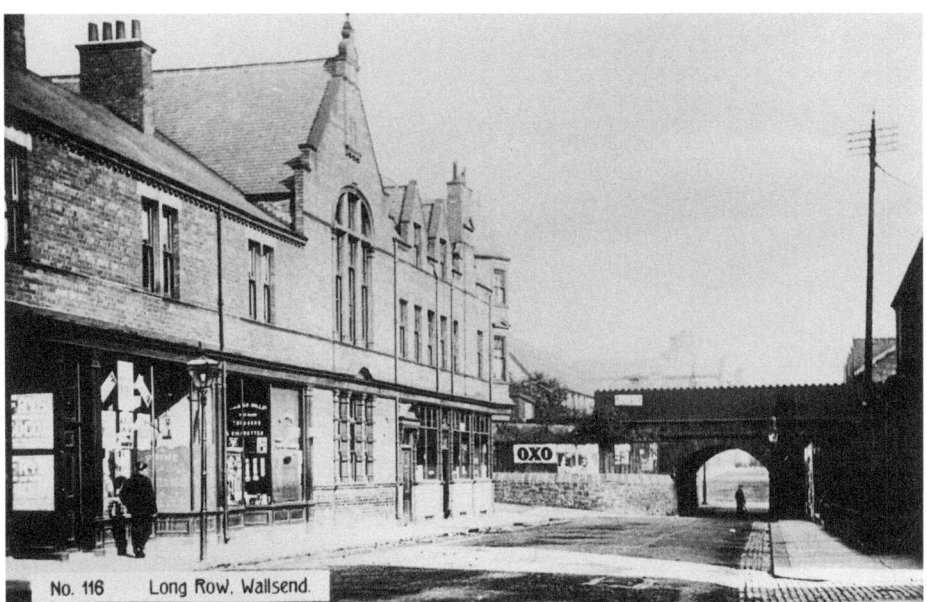

This was commonly known as The Ship Inn on Gainers Terrace during the 1950s, when this photograph was taken. Situated beside Swan Hunter's Shipyard, the pub in recent times has been known as the Ship in the Hole. In the background, to the right, is The Dock public house, fronting Gainers Terrace.

The Dock public house, Gainers Terrace, 1985. This photograph was taken shortly before it was destroyed by fire. The renamed Ship in the Hole is situated behind.

six
Shipbuilding

The *Turbinia* in the 1920s. Following the success of the *Turbinia* at the Spit Head Naval Review in 1897, when she recorded an impressive 31 knots to the astonishment of onlookers, the Turbinia Works at Wallsend were built. Charles Parson set up the Marine Steam Turbine Co. Ltd on the riverside off Davy Bank.

The spectacular launch of the SS *Mauretania*, the largest ship in the world, at Swan Hunter's on 20 September 1906. The *Mauretania* was the largest passenger ship to be built on the Tyne.

SS *Tynesider* and *Mauretania* in 1907. The photograph shows the *Mauretania* being fitted out in 1907 while being passed by the *Tynesider*, a steamer, also built at Wallsend. The *Mauretania* left the Tyne on 22 October 1907 and held the speed record for crossing the Atlantic for twenty-two years, to great local pride.

The launching of the *Venezia* on 30 April 1907, a French emigrant steamer built for Messrs Cyprian Fabre & Co., in Marseilles. The Revd Canon Green carried out a benedictory service before the launch.

Mrs A.P. Cole is pictured before the launch of the naval destroyer, *Hyperion*, at Swan Hunter's shipyard on 8 April 1936. She is seen here with Mr John Denham Christie, a director of Swan Hunter's.

This photograph shows the launch of the *Dominion Monarch* on 27 July 1938. She was the largest ship built on the Tyne by Swan Hunter's after the *Mauretania*. She was built specifically for the Shaw, Savill & Albion Line to sail to New Zealand via the Cape to carry 517 passengers and to bring back lamb and butter in the refrigerated hold.

Opposite below: The launch of the *Hyperion*, 8 April 1936. She was one of five naval ships launched on the Tyne that year. She was sunk on 22 December 1940, a mere four years later.

SS *Meduana*, Swan Hunter's, *c.* 1920. The French passenger and cargo-liner was launched at Wallsend on 30 September 1920 and is seen here being fitted out.

SS *Meduana*, Swan Hunter's, Wallsend, after the fire of 22 November 1920. The ship's hold caught fire and, during the fire-fighting exercise, the ship keeled over on to its side. Two men were killed.

Atlantic Conveyor, Swan Hunter's, 1985. This is taken from within the recently built Wooley Street housing development, with the *Atlantic Conveyor* dominating the Roman Fort.

Swan Hunter's dry dock in Wallsend was first built in 1885 as the River Tyne Dry Dock Engineering & Boilermaker Co. and is photographed here around 1911.

Swan Hunter's and Wigham Richardson's Neptune Yard in the 1930s. The office block in the background is on Benton Way, which led down to the Hebburn Ferry.

Tyne Shipyards, Wallsend, c. 1920. The North Eastern Marine Engineering Co. Ltd crane was built in 1909 and was said to be the biggest in the world. It stood an awesome 154ft high and could lift 150 tons from its 245ft-long horizontal jib. The crane became a listed building in 1990 but, following a Public Local Inquiry, permission was given to demolish it.

Hammerhead crane, North Eastern Marine, in 1985. The North Eastern Marine Engineering Co. Ltd was established in Wallsend in 1882. They occupied the site for over 100 years before being taken over by AMEC. The company built houses for its workers beside St Peter's church.

Wallsend Slipway & Engineering Co. Works, *c.* 1920. This picture was taken from Willington Gut looking west, with the North Eastern Marine crane in the background. Wallsend Slipway began in 1871 to repair ships using 1,000ft-long slipways. In 1905 the company began to build steam turbines and the turbines for the *Mauretania* were built here. The company closed in the early 1980s.

Crane, Wallsend Slipway, *c.* 1910. The 180-ton electric hammerhead crane featured here was built in 1910.

The *Franconia* was launched at Swan Hunter's and is seen here at Wallsend Slipway in 1910. She could carry 300 first class, 350 second class and 2,200 third class passengers, and her maiden voyage from Liverpool to New York was on 25 February 1911. She was used as a troop carrier during the First World War. and in 1916 she was torpedoed by a submarine and sank with the loss of twelve lives.

Wallsend Slipway workshop, *c.* 1912. A view from inside the workshop – the machinery is waiting to be moved and installed in a vessel.

The Wallsend Slipway workshop pictured here, *c.* 1915. The diesel engines shown are destined for use in a submarine and are nearing completion.

Wallsend Slipway crane under Willington Viaduct, *c.* 1984. The original Willington Viaduct was built in timber in 1839. It was rebuilt in cast iron in the later part of the century and eventually had to be strengthened and reinforced in the early 1980s before the Metro opened.

The Ferry in Wallsend-on-Tyne, *c.* 1920. It was situated at the foot of Benton Way, linking Wallsend to Hebburn.

Above: Hebburn Ferry, Wallsend, *c.* 1930. The ferries operated from 1904 until 1986, mainly serving shipyard workers.

Left: Here a Wallsend Corporation lorry loads a refuse hopper on the river in the 1930s. Wallsend's domestic waste was dumped at sea for many years, until environmental legislation put an end to this activity.

seven
Mining

Wallsend Colliery, c. 1900. The G and H Pits were situated to the south of St Peter's church, close to the present Hadrian Metro Station on the south of the Metro line. The Wallsend & Hebburn Coal Co. worked the coal from 1891 after Cornish pumping engines had been set up to pump water from the collieries, which had been flooded out in the 1850s. The reservoirs in the foreground were north of the railway track and east of Limekiln Road.

The pit head gear used for lowering and raising men and coal is seen in the centre of this photograph showing the Wallsend Colliery G and H Pits, c.1900.

This photograph reveals a derailed train at the church pit reservoir in 1905. The accident happened on 27 June 1905, when a North East Railway train collided with coal trucks. The driver and stoker were thrown into the water but were not injured.

Following the closure of the G Pit in 1934, the Rising Sun was the last colliery in Wallsend. Pictured here in the 1940s, the colliery produced 650,000 tons of coal a year and employed 1,750 men at its peak in 1964, before closing soon afterwards on 26 April 1969.

Opposite above: The new colliery, Wallsend, *c.* 1906. The picture shows the Rising Sun Colliery before it was opened in 1906. It took over two years to reach the Bensham seam. A second shaft was opened in 1915 to allow the colliery to operate independently from the G Pit.

Opposite below: Wallsend Miners Hall, Station Road, in the 1940s. While it was built in 1925 as the Wallsend G and Rising Sun Collieries Welfare Institute, in recent years it has been used as a snooker club.

Old colliery houses at Wallsend (now Carville Road), c. 1895. These houses were typical of miners' cottages, which were built in rows close to the colliery. These cottages were built just to the north of A and B Pits, close to Segedunum Roman Fort. William Crister would have lived in such a cottage. William Crister was 'The Wallsend Miner', the main subject of a book written by the Revd W. Everitt in 1835 following his death in the 1835 Wallsend Colliery Disaster. William Crister was a popular lay preacher at the Carville chapel, despite having no formal education.

Opposite above: The plaque to the memory of the 102 men and boys killed in the 1835 Wallsend Colliery Disaster, St Peter's churchyard, 1994. Wallsend Local History Society campaigned to have the plaque erected with help from the National Union of Mineworkers, Northumberland Area and the North Tyneside Metropolitan Borough Council. A book to commemorate the disaster, written by the author and his wife Pauline Hutchinson, was also published that year by North Tyneside Libraries on behalf of the Wallsend Local History Society.

Opposite below: Cllr Bob Usher, Mayor of North Tyneside, is pictured in St Peter's churchyard on 18 June 1994. The mayor was about to unveil the plaque to commemorate the forgotten miners from the 1835 Wallsend Colliery Disaster who were buried in an unmarked grave. Also in the photograph is Mr Vincent Wallace, the late Chairman of Wallsend Local History Society.

18 June
1835
In memory of
102 men and boys
(8 - 76 years)
who lost their lives in the
Wallsend Colliery Disaster
erected by Wallsend
L.H.S. N.T.M.B.C. N.U.M.
Northumberland Area
1994

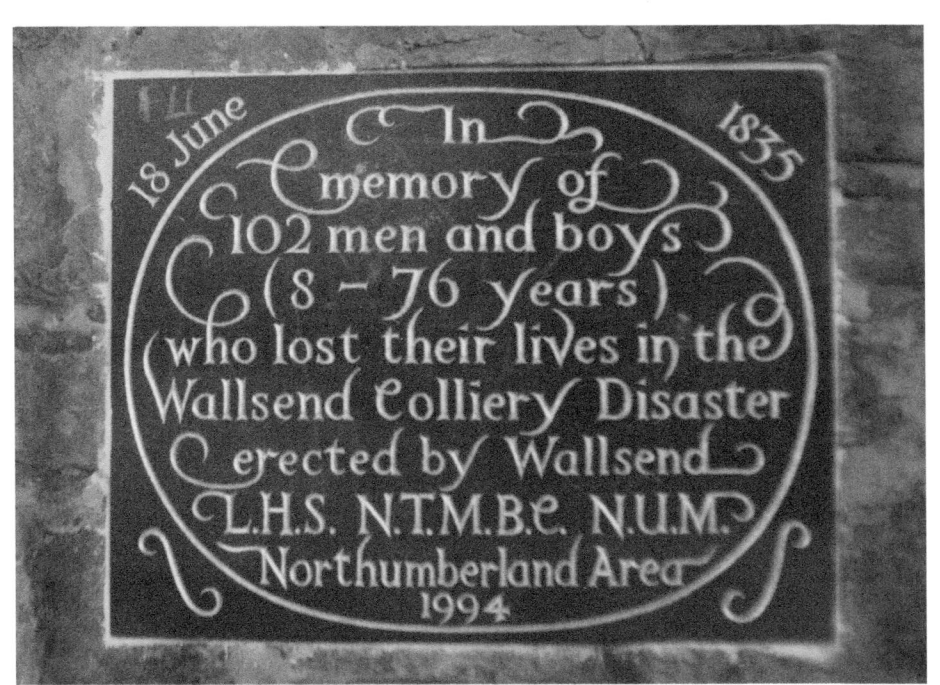

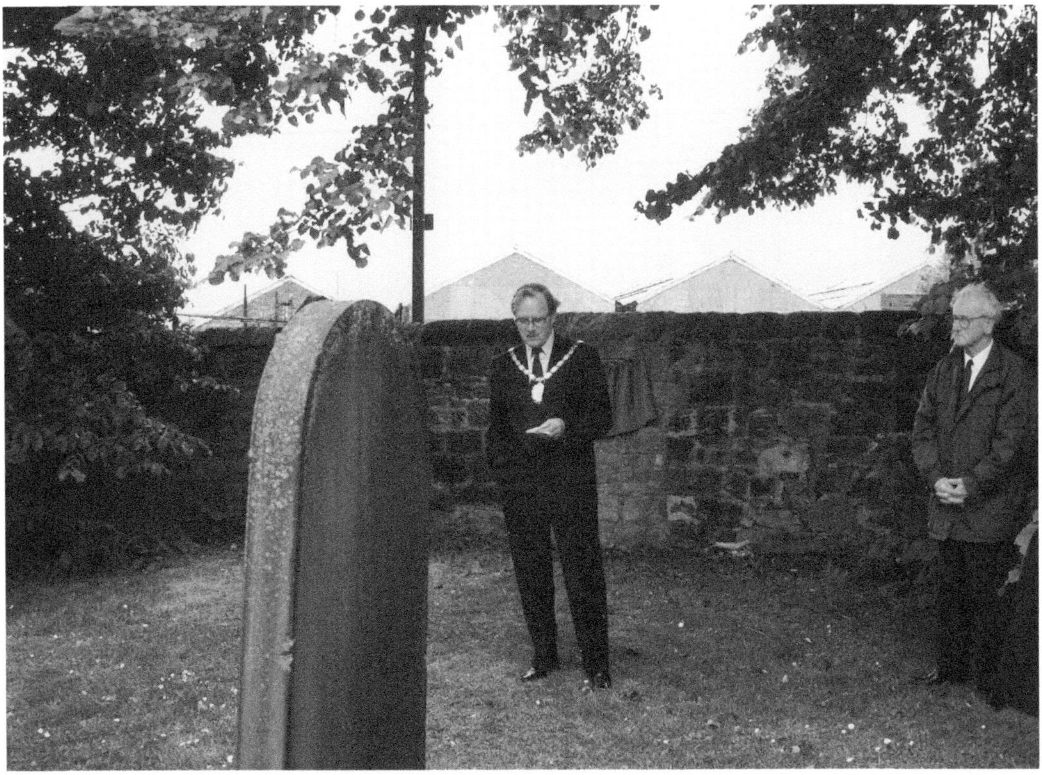

The G Pit in Wallsend, *c.* 1985. The site is immediately to the west of Hadrian Metro Station fronting Hadrian Road. On the right, below the NEM crane, is the concrete cap which covers the pit shaft.

Bigges Main, Wallsend-on-Tyne, *c.* 1910. A tram from Gosforth is travelling south towards Wallsend along the route of the old Coxlodge wagon way. This is now the main road to the Wallsend Sports Centre known as Rheydt Avenue and the village of Bigges Main is seen in the background.

West Row, Bigges Main, *c.* 1910. Bigges Main was a mining village situated close to where Wallsend Sports Centre now stands. A colliery was built here after 1785 with three shafts to the Main Seam. The landowner was Thomas Charles Bigge and the village built to serve the colliery was known as Bigges Main. The colliery was abandoned in 1856 when all the collieries in the area were flooded out.

Rheydt Avenue in 1974, following the line of the old Coxlodge wagon way to Wallsend Sports Centre which is built on the site of the former village of Bigges Main.

The Masons Arms, seen here in 1967, was the last building to be demolished in Bigges Main village before the Wallsend Sports Centre opened in 1970 and the Wallsend Golf Club in 1973.

The Masons Arms, Bigges Main, c. 1960. George Hunter was listed as one of the last landlords, having taken over in 1929 from Emilie Annie Elliott who held the licence from 1906.

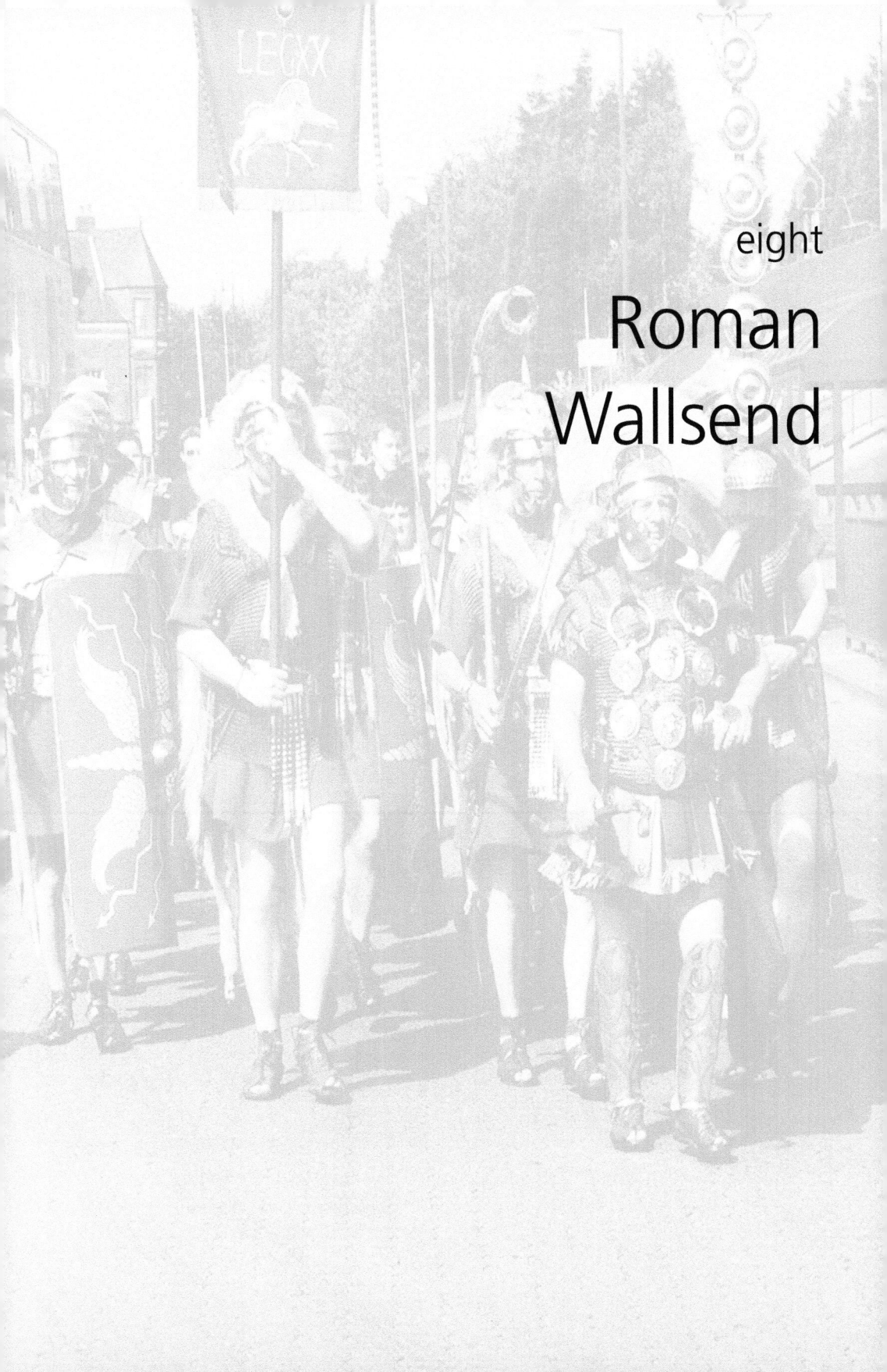

eight

Roman Wallsend

Simpson's Hotel in Buddle Street, here photographed in around 1916, was built in 1912 during which the remains of the east gate of Segedunum Roman Fort were found and were moved to Wallsend Park to be displayed. The hotel was named after Dr Robert Simpson of Newcastle and had over 300 rooms to house the transient workers it was built to serve.

Photographed here around the same time as the above picture, this view of Simpson's Hotel looks west along Buddle Street. The plaque on the corner of the hotel in Hunter Street was erected to record that it was at this point that the remains of the east gate of Segedunum Roman Fort were found in 1912.

The closure of Simpson's Hotel occured in 1981 (around the time of this photograph); it was later demolished in 1983.

Segedunum Roman Fort, 1985. Following excavations in the early 1980s, the land was back-filled and the position of the fort walls and towers marked out on the new surface by decorative paving. In the foreground is the newly marked out south-east angle tower with the line of the fort wall extending northwards, and to the right the Swan Hunter's canteen is visible.

Also taken in 1985, this photograph of the Segedunum Roman wall shows the position of the branch wall, which led to the Tyne from the south-east corner of the fort and was marked by decorative stonework.

These are the remains of the branch wall in Swan Hunter's shipyard in 1984. Following the discovery of the branch wall during excavations for the *Mauritania*'s berth in 1903, some of the stones were kept and displayed in the shipyard close to where they were found. Above the stones a plaque explains their significance. Swan Hunter's main office block is seen in the distance on the far right.

Headquarters building, Segedunum Roman Fort, 1985. Following excavations in the early 1980s, the soil was replaced on site to the present-day level, with the exception of the Headquarters building. The remains of the Headquarters building are seen in the foreground and Rawdon Court is seen in the background beyond Buddle Street.

Here the remains of the Headquarters building, Segedunum, are in front of the *Atlantic Conveyor* in 1985.

The public clock in Wallsend-on-Tyne standing on the corner of Station Road and Buddle Street, c. 1910. The large building behind the clock was used as a doctors surgery and offices before it became the Wallsend Heritage Centre. The building was opened in 1986, but only remained open for a few years. It was later used as a base for archaeologists during the excavations in the 1990s of the fort prior to the opening of the present museum in 2000.

Swan Hunter's Institute Building, 1986. Standing at the top of Swan's Bank, the building now forms part of the new museum. The low building between the Institute Building and the canteen was originally constructed as a shooting range before the canteen was built. The clock on the corner is a listed building and previously occupied a site on the opposite corner to the north of Buddle Street, before it was moved for traffic safety reasons.

This plaque, north of Buddle Street in 1985, records the position of a Roman wall. It was erected in the 1930s on the grounds of Carville chapel to record where the remains of the Roman wall were found under the surface. The plaque survived the demolition of Carville chapel in the mid-1970s and has since been moved into the museum.

Reconstruction of the Roman wall, Buddle Street, 1997. The photograph shows, from left to right: Graham Stobbs, Ken Hall, John Jackson and Peter Hutchinson, who, together with the author, were some of the original volunteer Wallsend Heritage Guides established in 1986.

This is the official opening of the reconstructed section of the Roman wall on 5 June 1997, where the deputy mayor, Cllr Arlene Richardson, unveils a tablet to record the event.

Wall reconstruction opening ceremony, 5 June 1997. The original line of Hadrian's Wall is indicated by the remains of the foundations; these have been preserved and consolidated. The new wall had to be set back from the original foundations to preserve the original structure.

The deputy mayor, Cllr Arlene Richardson, prepares to pose for a photograph with a Roman soldier at the groundbreaking ceremony when work commenced on the tower at Segedunum on 5 June 1997.

Roman soldiers march from Segedunum Fort on 17 June 2000, almost 2,000 years after the original fort was used in Wallsend. As part of the opening celebrations for the new museum, the Ermine Street Guard Re-enactment Group march to Wallsend Metro Station from outside the fort.

Left: Stunned passengers in the Metro trams got quite a surprise when the train pulled into Wallsend Metro Station, as the Roman soldiers from the re-enactment group wait for the Metro to arrive on 17 June 2000.

Opposite
Above: This photograph captures a sacrifice to the gods at the opening ceremony of the new Segedunum Roman Museum on 17 June 2000.

Below left: 'I don't care who you are, you still need a ticket to get in!' The security was extremely tight at Segedunum Roman Museum on 17 June 2000.

Below right: Crowds mingle with Roman soldiers and dignitaries under the new tower at the Opening Day at Segedunum Roman Museum, 17 June 2000.

The Roman soldiers escort guests and visitors through Wallsend Bus Station, 17 June 2000.

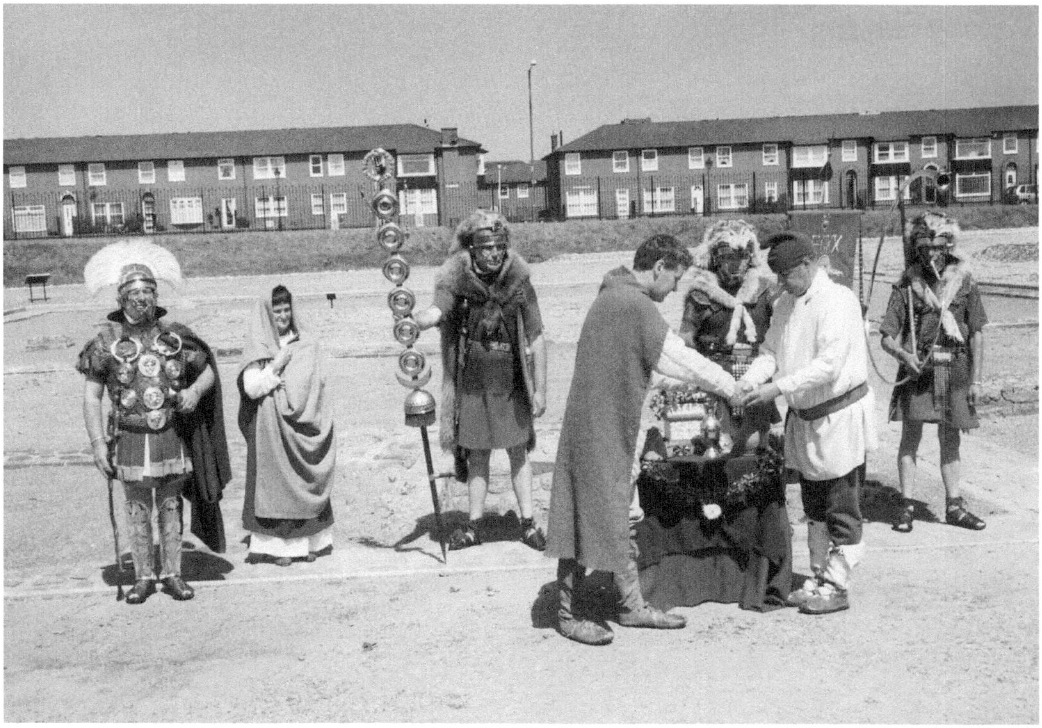

Other local titles published by The History Press

Jarrow Then & Now
Paul Perry

This selection of over 80 photographs of Jarrow charts the changes in the town over the last century. Capturing in detail the effects of modernisation good, bad, and indifferent, *Jarrow: Then & Now* will appeal to all those who know the area.
ISBN 0-7524-1588-3

Newcastle-Upon-Tyne
Peter Hepplewhite

Produced in conjunction with the Tyne & Wear archive service, this collection of 200 old photographs offers images of a changing city. With scenes of transport, industry, sport and recreation, this book will be a memorable read for all of those who know Newcastle.
ISBN: 0-7524-1598-0

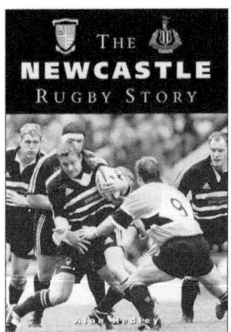

The Newcastle Rugby Story
Alan Hedley

Rugby in the North-East has a long history and intertwined with it is the story of the Newcastle club. This book traces the 123-year history from the founding of Gosforth through its great victories and decline and the subsequent transformation into the Falcons, as they are now universally known.
ISBN: 0-7524-2046-1

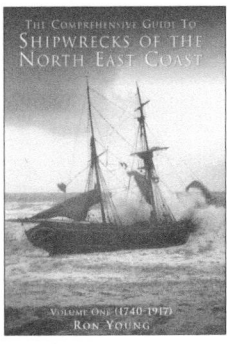

The Comprehensive Guide to Shipwrecks of the North-East Coast
(Volume one 1740-1917)
Ron Young

Spanning an impressive time period, this book, by experienced diver Ron Young, catalogues the histories of the ships that have been stranded and wrecked along the North-East coast of England. A fascinating and informative read.
ISBN: 0-7524-1749-5

If you are interested in purchasing other books published by The History Press, or in case you have difficulty finding any of our books in your local bookshop, you can also place orders directly through our website

www.thehistorypress.co.uk